# ARE WE THE PEOPLE?

How We the People

Can Take Charge of

Our Constitution

James W. Lucas

ISBN-13: 978-1478155393

ISBN-10: 1478155396

Constitution Renewal Initiative

www.TimelyRenewed.com

cover by StudioBridger

# TABLE OF CONTENTS

Introduction                                                          3

1.    The Amendment Process:  How It Died,
      and How It Can Be Revived                                        6

2.    Why Revive the Amendment Process?                               17

3.    Making the People the 'Real Show':
      How the Amendment Amendment Would Work                          26

4.    Why Keep State Equality in Ratification?                        34

5.    Why Not Call an Article Five Convention?                        41

6.    Why Democrats, Republicans and Americans
      Should Support the Amendment Amendment                          53

Appendix: Text of the Amendment Amendment                            58

# INTRODUCTION

*The candid citizen must confess that if the policy of the government, upon vital questions, affecting the whole people, is to be irrevocably fixed by decisions of the Supreme Court, the instant they are made, in ordinary litigation between parties, in personal actions, the people will have ceased to be their own rulers, having, to that extent, practically resigned their government into the hands of that eminent tribunal.*

*This country, with its institutions, belongs to the people who inhabit it. Whenever they shall grow weary of the existing government, they can exercise their constitutional right of amending it. ... I will venture to add that, to me, the convention mode seems preferable, in that it allows amendments to originate with the people themselves, instead of only permitting them to take or reject, propositions, originated by others.*

*Why should there not be a patient confidence in the ultimate justice of the people? Is there any better, or equal hope, in the world? ... We are not enemies, but friends. We must not be enemies. Though passion may have strained, it must not break our bonds of affection. The mystic chords of memory, stretching from every battle-field, and patriot grave, to every living heart and hearthstone, all over this broad land, will yet swell the chorus of the Union, when again touched, as surely they will be, by the better angels of our nature.*

*Abraham Lincoln, 1861*

Five-to-Four. Five-to-Four. Again and again, down to us they come, decisions of the Supreme Court, often by one-vote margins, decisions deciding big issues for we 335 million Americans. Must all states perform same-sex marriages? Can states take account of race in college admissions? Can Congress force you to buy something? (The answer to the last is no, but it can tax you to force you to buy it, a conclusion decreed by a single Supreme Court justice.) And on it goes.

3

Consider two famous Supreme Court decisions: *Citizens United v. FEC* and *Roe v. Wade*. The conventional wisdom says that if you love one of these Supreme Court decisions you hate the other. In *Citizens United* the Supreme Court declared that corporations are people with First Amendment free speech rights, and therefore overturned laws which limited most corporate spending on elections. In *Roe* the Supreme Court declared that fetuses are not people with Fifth Amendment protections against the taking of life, and therefore overturned laws which limited most abortions.

And, of course, all Supreme Court decisions are subject to the political roll of the dice depending on which President wins the lottery and is able to name more justices, as vividly shown by the recent decision in *Dobbs v. Jackson Women's Health Organization*, which overturned *Roe v. Wade*. Regardless of your view of the *Roe* and *Dobbs* decisions, it is clear that the issue of access to abortion turned on the fact that former casino owner Donald Trump was able to appoint three justices to the Supreme Court, whereas many Presidents end up appointing none.

Regardless of your view of these decisions, they have one very important thing in common. In both the Supreme Court declared that the status and rights of both corporations and fetuses are to be found in the Constitution. Yet, the Constitution itself says nothing about either corporations or fetuses. What you do see are those first three words, WE THE PEOPLE.

You are one of the People. But the Supreme Court has declared that your vote and everyone else's votes and the votes of all the legislators you elect do not count. The only votes that count are those of five Supreme Court justices. In our presidential elections it often seems that the most important thing the President does is to appoint Supreme Court justices. This is because once the Supreme Court says something is in the Constitution, even if it isn't there, the

Court's declaration is fixed and final unless the Supreme Court itself changes it. As things stand now, no act of Congress, the President, or any state or any American can effectively change a Supreme Court decision. Is this any way to run a Constitution?

This short book asks this question. Shouldn't we the People be making fundamental decisions like these? If you look at the Constitution, it says nothing about the Supreme Court being the ultimate arbiter of its meaning. Instead, it provides that the last word should be with us, the People. The mechanism for exercising that power is our right of amendment. However, that right is now moribund. It has been over a hundred years since the People decided a major constitutional issue by the democratic process of amendment. Why has the amendment process died, and can it be revived? This book is about how we can reform the amendment process to get back our right to say what our Constitution means.

Abraham Lincoln famously described our government as "of the people, by the people, and for the people." But in his first inaugural address, quoted above, he warned that if the Supreme Court became the final arbiter of the Constitution's meaning "the people will have ceased to be their own rulers" and will have "resigned their government into the hands of that eminent tribunal." Was Abraham Lincoln right? Do this country and its institutions really belong to the people who inhabit it? Do the People rule, or the judges? What if you, as one of the People, were presented with this proposition:

*It is proposed that an unelected permanent committee of five elite lawyers have the power to amend the Constitution any time that, in their sole opinion, they feel it needs to be updated.*

How would you vote?

# ONE

## The Amendment Process:
## How It Died, and How It Can Be Revived

Of course, the Constitution can not explicitly cover every eventuality, and someone has to decide situations where the Constitution is silent. Many argue that that someone has to be the Supreme Court. But that is wrong. The framers of the Constitution knew very well that they had not covered everything, and that new situations would arise that they had not foreseen. However, the framers' solution was not to let five unelected, life-tenured and unaccountable lawyers decide. Instead, the framers' solution to these situations was Article Five of the Constitution.

Article Five sets out the procedures for amending the Constitution. However, if you are under the age of 60, you probably have no memory of the Constitution being amended. And you would have to be over 100 years old to remember the last time a really major constitutional issue was resolved by formal amendment. The last regular amendment to the Constitution, the 26th lowering the voting age by a couple of years to 18, was enacted in 1971.[1] The last amendment with major lasting national impact was the 19th giving all women the right to vote. It became effective in 1920.

There are two main reasons why the framers' method of updating the Constitution has become moribund. The first is basic logistics. To amend the Constitution using Article Five, you must first

---

[1] The 27th Amendment involving congressional pay raises became effective in 1992. However, that was a peculiar case where part of the original 1791 Bill of Rights had lain dormant for two centuries until it was revived by a campaign to complete its ratification.

pass an amendment by two-thirds vote in both Houses of Congress, and then it must be ratified by three fourths of the states. Getting five votes on the Supreme Court is far simpler than the approval of thousands of legislators in dozens of legislatures.

The second is more subtle. Amendment by litigation before the Supreme Court is the province of the elites. Expensive and prestigious attorneys press cases through the court system, where they are decided by other prestigious attorneys aided by law clerks who aspire some day themselves to be prestigious attorneys and judges. It is all very contained within the elite, and unlikely to produce any results of which the political and economic elites disapprove. In contrast, getting an amendment approved under Article Five, if it ever happened, would be a purely democratic political process, open to grassroots pressure and enthusiasm. Who knows what the People might pass?

### An Amendment Amendment to Revive the Amendment Process

And that's the point. We need to reform Article Five so that we the People can decide what our Constitution means, not five unelected and unaccountable judges. The Appendix of this book sets out a specific proposal to accomplish this. Rather unimaginatively called the "Amendment Amendment," it provides that amendments to the Constitution could be initiated in either of two ways:

1)      A vote of five eighths of both houses of Congress (that's 62.5% instead of the current two thirds or 66 $2/_3$%),  or

2)      at least five states acting within 120 days of each other.

Once initiated, amendments could be ratified in either of two ways:

1)      Approval by two thirds of the states with a majority of the U.S. population (including the five or more initiating states), or

2)      approval by five eighths of the states and a vote of five eighths of both houses of Congress (but a second vote by Congress would be unnecessary if the amendment was initiated by Congress).

The current Article Five requires ratification by three-fourths of the states (38 of 50, the most difficult requirement in the world) whereas two-thirds is 34 of 50 states and five-eighths is 32 of 50 states.

The specific text in the Appendix contains a number of other provisions to facilitate the amendment process and clear up various issues which have arisen over the last 235 years under the current Article Five. These are all explained later on.

Now, you may look at this and say, where did those wacky numbers come from? You can ask why this proposal is better than any number of other ways we might reform the amendment process. You might ask why the proposal drops the other half of the current Article Five, the unused provision allowing two thirds of the states to call a convention to propose amendments. And you should ask if this is really needed. To answer all these questions, we have to take a quick trip back, and begin at the beginning.

### The Origins and Fall of the People's Amendment Power

If the framers of the Constitution wanted the People acting through their democratically elected legislatures to make fundamental decisions about the Constitution's meaning by amendment, why did they make amendment by Article Five so difficult, and amendment by the Supreme Court so easy? The short answer to both is that they didn't mean to in either case.

When the grand federal convention convened in the summer of 1787, the only existing written constitutions in the entire world were the constitutions of the newly independent American states which had been written just a few years before by, among others, many of the same men who were now assembling in Philadelphia. It was universally agreed at the outset that whatever they were writing should be subject to amendment. Some of the new state constitutions provided various means of amendment, but they ran all over the lot in terms of requirements and procedures. The very idea that a national constitution might be amendable was novel. Previous comprehensive governing laws were supposedly unchangeable. For example, one did not amend the Bible!

Various methods of amendment were knocked around in the early days of the convention. One proposal was that the states could call a new convention to propose amendments, but that was quickly shot down by none other than James Madison. In his terse notes, the man who is known as the "Father of the Constitution," summarized his objections as "How was a Convention to be formed? by what rule decide? what the force of its acts?" Instead Madison introduced a proposal dropping the convention, and simply providing that the "Legislature of the U--- S--- … could propose amendments of its own initiative" or "on the application of two thirds of the Legislatures of the several States."

The 1787 convention adopted Madison's suggestion. That would have been the amendment provision of the Constitution except for events on the second to last day of the convention, September 15, 1787 (the convention concluded on September 17, which has since been known as Constitution Day). George Mason of Virginia declared that he still mistrusted this new national government. Mason was sure that the national government would grow far beyond the framers' original vision and become ever more powerful and oppressive.

Whether one looks on Mason as a pioneer defender of democracy and civil liberties or as a sort of proto-MAGA populist, whether your poison is warrantless searches by federal agents under the PATRIOT Act or the requirement that individuals pay a tax penalty for not buying health insurance under the Affordable Care Act, all sides of the political spectrum would agree that Mason had a point. Among other fears, he did not think the new national Congress could be trusted to send amendments requested by the states out for ratification. Over Madison's objections, some other delegates re-introduced the idea of having the states propose amendments through a convention. So near to the end of their great project, and after four long hot summer months of debate, Madison acquiesced in the move, but still presciently warned "that difficulties might arise as to the form, the quorum &c. which in Constitutional regulations ought to be as much as possible avoided."

For Mason, this turned out to be a classic case of the perfect being an enemy of the good. An amending convention has never been held, nor is one likely to ever occur for reasons which will be discussed below. The result has been exactly what Mason was trying to avoid. The Constitution has become the exclusive property of two bodies of the national government, Congress and the Supreme Court. Without a realistic convention alternative, Congress has a practical monopoly – unused now for over half a century – on launching constitutional amendment proposals.

Much of the blame for this situation can be attributed to Congress' gridlock and pre-occupation with other matters. However, another problem is simply numbers. At the beginning there were 13 states, 26 Senators and 64 members of the House of Representatives. Thus the votes of 18 Senators and 43 Representatives were required to initiate an amendment and ten states had to ratify it. Today those numbers are 67 Senators, 290 Representatives and 38 states. Simple common experience tells us that the larger the group, the harder it is to reach unanimity. Getting ten people to all agree where to go to dinner is difficult, but getting 38 people to all agree and show up is impossible.

This phenomenon has actually been analyzed by statistical scientists and formalized as the law of large numbers. Statisticians and law professors Rosalind Dixon and Richard Holden have applied this statistical analysis to the United States Constitution's amendment process. They concluded that, for a modern amendment proposal to have the same statistical likelihood of ratification as when the Constitution first came into effect, the three-fourth (75%) and two-thirds (67%) requirements would have to be reduced to 62%.

Absent the realistic possibility of congressional initiation of amendments, now the Supreme Court effectively has the exclusive power to change the Constitution, a power no where authorized in the Constitution itself and subject only to the justices' own self-restraint.

### *The Rise of Judicial Amendment*

This rise in the power of the Supreme Court has a long and complicated history. It began in 1803 with the case of *Marbury v. Madison*, which established that the Supreme Court could invalidate an act of Congress which violated the Constitution. However, the Supreme Court did not act again against an act of Congress until the *Dred Scott* case in 1857, which upheld the status of slavery in free states. Universally regarded as one of, if not the, worst Supreme Court decisions in the nation's history, it helped bring on the Civil War, and was criticized by Lincoln in his first inaugural. Despite this unhappy precedent, after the Civil War, and especially after the adoption of the vaguely worded 14th Amendment in 1868, the Supreme Court became much more active in invoking the Constitution against both state and federal laws. For example, in the 1880s the Court began to declare that corporations are persons entitled to constitutional protection from

11

state laws under the 14<sup>th</sup> Amendment. This is the legal doctrine underlying the *Citizens United* decision.

That trend has continued to the present time. Up until the 1930s the Supreme Court overturned many economic regulations. After 1937 and the appointment of justices by Franklin Roosevelt, the Court did an about-face and upheld all government regulation. In both periods the results were supposedly based on reading the Constitution. Beginning in the 1960s the Court began to find many more new rights in the Constitution, such as *Roe v. Wade*'s right to access to abortion. More recently progressive law professors have accused the Court under Chief Justices Rehnquist and Roberts of distorting the Constitution to again make many pro-business decisions like *Citizens United*.

"Judicial activism" is one of those terms, like "cult" or "slut," that mainly just tells you that the user does not like the particular religion, woman or court decision they're throwing the term at. But there is a real issue underlying the term. Regardless of what you think about the Supreme Court's decisions over these last 150 years, one effect is indisputable. The Supreme Court has generated tens of thousands of pages of rulings all supposedly mandated by our short dozen-page long Constitution. These rulings have effectively changed the meaning of our Constitution.

Many have justified this process by the need to adjust the Constitution with the times. An early example of this is the doctrine of corporate personhood developed in the 1880s to accommodate the rise of the modern business corporation. Whatever the adjustment, it is the Supreme Court which makes it. And with the amendment process moribund, there is no effective limit on this power of the Supreme Court, and of the elites who control it.

## A Court of the Elites, by the Elites, and for the Elites

The current personnel of the Supreme Court illustrate this elite control of the modern process of amendment by litigation. University of Tennessee law professor Benjamin Barton has analyzed the backgrounds of all of the Supreme Court justices since the beginning of the nation. He found that the modern Supreme Court differs significantly from earlier Supreme Courts. For example, historically, every Supreme Court included at least one, if not several, justices who had served in an elected office. Indeed, one Chief Justice, William Howard Taft, was a former President of the United States. Yet since Sandra Day O'Connor's retirement in 2006, none of the Supreme Court justices has ever held public office.

Historically judges, including Supreme Court justices, were named from the ranks of working lawyers. Prior to the present time, Supreme Court justices had an average of sixteen years of law practice experience. The average on the current court is only six years of actual experience practicing law. And most of that experience has been in highly specialized work appealing cases to circuit courts and the Supreme Court. In former times, the idea of a judge, even a Supreme Court justice, who had never himself tried a case would have been laughable. Today it is the norm.

So, if they have not been working as regular lawyers or serving in elected office, what have the current justices been doing before coming on the Supreme Court? Basically, they have been working as either law professors, government lawyers, or as appellate court judges.

The changes are geographical as well. The current court has a greater concentration of justices from the Northeast than at any time in American history. Even in the beginning, when the nation was only the East Coast, there were always some southerners on the Court. The one exception to this concentration on the Northeast is time spent in

Washington, D.C., where the current justices have spent more time in their careers than was the case for any previous Court.

Another striking contrast with all earlier Courts is that every member of the current Court is a product of Yale or Harvard law schools. And despite the proliferation of colleges and universities over the course of U.S. history, the current justices have the highest proportion of elite undergraduate educations of any Court in history.

Barton argues that this rarified background has resulted in decisions which are too complicated and nuanced to be useful, and too frequently divided among pluralities and dissents without clear, straight-forward majority opinions. He attributes this to the justices' lack of practical, real-life experience in client-based law practice or politics, where one learns that sometimes it is better to compromise to get a definitive result, and how difficult it is to work with complicated abstract judicial rulings. In contrast, for legal academics and appellate judges the more obtuse one's reasoning the better, and going your own way is rewarded over cooperation.

One way to illustrate this phenomenon is the length of Supreme Court opinions. *Brown v. Board of Education*, the 1954 case outlawing school segregation, and certainly one of the most important Supreme Court decisions in the nation's history, was all of ten pages long. However, in the 1960s and 1970s average opinion length leapt as the Supreme Court began to be much more aggressive in asserting its right to new constitutional interpretation. Thus, *Roe v. Wade* in 1973 was 63 pages long including a concurrence and dissent. However, the current Court's opinions are the longest by far. For example, in 2010 *Citizens United* weighed in at a mind-numbing 183 pages and the *Dobbs* decision in 2022 overruling *Roe v. Wade* totaled 205 pages.

*Brown v. Board of Education* illustrates the importance of real-world experience in another way. The decision was unanimous, which legal historians agree contributed immensely to its long-term acceptance. Historians also agree that that unanimous vote was largely the work of Chief Justice Earl Warren in cajoling his fellow justices into supporting the decision. Warren's success in this undoubtedly drew upon the former California Governor's years of political experience in getting consensus though compromise and backroom persuasion, virtues in politics which are anathema in academe.

The modern practice of letting the Supreme Court adjust the Constitution means that these academic traits are now seeping into our constitutional law. To understand what simple phrases like "due process of law" or "establishment of religion" mean requires a deep knowledge of dozens of complicated Supreme Court decisions. In a famous speech on Constitution Day in 1937, Franklin Roosevelt declared that the Constitution should be "a layman's document, not a lawyer's contract." Nowadays even most lawyers can be hard-pressed to understand the Court's opinions.

Another problem with letting the amendment process go dormant and relying exclusively on the Supreme Court to update the Constitution is that there are some things that even the most free-wheeling Supreme Court can not change. The written text is simply too clear to work around. For example, if you feel that Presidents should be elected by direct popular vote instead of the Electoral College system, so that we do not have a repeat of the 2000 election where George W. Bush was elected (with the help of the Supreme Court) even though he received fewer total votes than Al Gore, constitutional amendment is the only sure permanent way to make that happen.[2] This issue was raised again in the 2016 election, where

---

[2] There is a proposal to have states with a majority of electoral votes agree to vote for the national popular vote winner, but it is almost certainly unconstitutional. That popular vote advocates feel that they must resort to

Donald Trump won the Electoral College vote while receiving almost three million fewer votes than Hillary Clinton.

Or, if you look at our $35 trillion plus national debt, and feel that Congress should be required to balance its budget instead of running up ever-growing federal deficits for the rest of time, again constitutional amendment is the only sure permanent way to make that happen.[3]

Beyond these problems is a deeper concern. The United States of America is supposed to be a republic, a representative democracy. But what kind of democracy is it where five Harvard and Yale law school graduates with little practical real world experience can change the fundamental meaning of our foundational document, and change it without any appeal from their determination?

---

such a dubious measure is another example of frustration with the rigidity of Article Five's procedures.

[3] Electing fiscally conservative members of Congress may lead to a balanced budget during that Congress, but they can not prevent any future Congress from running up new debt.

# TWO

## Why Revive the Amendment Process?

Of course, many will claim that it isn't all so bad. What harm has been done by Congress and the Supreme Court's *de facto* monopolies on the meaning of our Constitution? Are *Citizens United* and *Roe v. Wade* really so bad, are the PATRIOT Act and endless federal budget deficits really such serious infringements on our rights and future that we need to amend the Constitution to deal with them? Don't we all realize what selfless public servants members of Congress are, and don't the Supreme Court justices all look so wise in their black robes sitting in their Grecian temple looking courthouse across from the Capitol in Washington, DC? Congress and the Supreme Court can be trusted to take care of you.

Or to take you. There are many different reasons why Americans have recently given Congress the lowest approval ratings since opinion polling began, and a majority feel that the Supreme Court's decisions are politically motivated. Undoubtedly many of those reasons may be in conflict. However, there are some propositions which seem to enjoy broad and consistent support. An opinion poll asking about the *Citizens United* decision found that 79% of respondents "support passage of an amendment to overturn the decision and make clear that corporations do not have the same rights as people." Another showed 65% in favor of a constitutional amendment allowing limits on the amount of personal funds a candidate may spend on her or his campaign as permitted by the Supreme Court's *Buckley v. Valeo* decision.

Constitutional amendments allowing restrictions on the role of money in political campaigns are not the only amendments which have enjoyed enduring popular support. Opinion polls in 1994 and 2011 reported 74% in favor of a balanced budget amendment, 76% support in 2005 and 80% in 2023, including over three fourths of Democrats and independents. In the 1980s, support for a balanced budget amendment was so great that 32 states requested a constitutional convention to propose it. (As will be discussed below, the fear of a runaway convention led the last states to hesitate short of the 34 state applications required by Article Five to call a convention.)

Another proposed amendment which has enjoyed long-term support is one to limit the number of terms members of Congress can serve. In the early 1990s many states enacted congressional term limits under state law, but these state laws were ruled unconstitutional by the Supreme Court in 1995. Nonetheless support for a term limits amendment has been steadily growing, from 71% in 2005 to 78% in 2010 to now (as of 2023) exceed 87% of all voters.

Despite this widespread and constant public support, balanced budget and term limits amendments have always failed to obtain the necessary two-thirds approvals in Congress. In the case of balanced budget amendment proposals, this has been despite continuing major drives for over four decades since the 1980s. And there is no indication that prospects are any better for the many proposals for an amendment to reverse the *Citizens United* decision.

Now, it may be that there are good reasons to not put these proposed amendments in the Constitution. The question is whether Congress should be making that determination. Congress has vested institutional interests at stake in each of these proposals. Overturning *Citizens United* could seriously disrupt the system upon which most members of Congress rely to finance their campaigns. A balanced budget amendment would curtail Congress' power to spend as much as it wants. And a term limits amendment would end the ability of members of Congress to make life-long careers as federal politicians, and their access to all of the power and perks that that brings.

All of these proposals would be far more likely to get a fair hearing if they could be introduced in the states first. The other delegates at the 1787 convention agreed with both Mason and Madison that the states should be able to initiate amendment proposals independent of Congress. The reasons why it is important that states be able to initiate amendments go deeper than a few popular proposals frustrated by Congress' self-interest. The Constitution is our fundamental law, and control of that fundamental law means control of our entire system of government. Although no member of Congress would be so impolitic as to say it bluntly, its *de facto* monopoly on initiating constitutional amendments gives Congress a tremendous power. Frank J. Sorauf, the distinguished University of Minnesota political scientist and a leading expert on campaign finance reform has said quite frankly that "it does not seem very likely that we shall ever see an Article V convention. Opposition to one runs very deep in the Congress, and it is not limited to one party or ideological stripe. Congressional fear of the unknown is great. Moreover, the Congress is jealous of its own powers and suspicious of what it cannot control. ... The Congress simply prefers to control the amending process."

Sorauf is a leading proponent of reasonable campaign finance reform, and provided expert testimony in defense of campaign finance reform laws in pre-*Citizens United* anti-reform lawsuits. However, his view of the matter has been echoed by none other than the late Antonin Scalia, the leading conservative voice on the Supreme Court and a member of the *Citizens United* majority. Speaking when he was still Professor Scalia of the University of Chicago, the combative conservative bluntly charged that Congress "likes the existing confusion, because that deters resort to the convention process. It does not want amending power to be anywhere but its own hands."

As we have seen, this congressional road block on amendments actually has left the Constitution in the hands of the Supreme Court.

This is a profoundly anti-democratic way to change our basic law, which begins with We The People, not We The Judges. Of course, sometimes we like particular Supreme Court decisions. In deciding what we think of this power of the Supreme Court, there is a temptation to tally up how many Supreme Court decisions we approve or disapprove, how many like *Citizens United* there have been versus how many like *Roe v. Wade*.

But that must not be the criterion. This argument is bigger than whether we like or dislike particular Supreme Court decisions. Democracy is not about a particular policy outcome. It is about the will of the people prevailing. Do we give up on democracy because we lose an election? As Lincoln warned, as soon as we let a few unelected, life-tenured, elite lawyers make basic decisions about the meaning of our most basic law, they are the rulers, not We The People. This is a structural issue about how we make our democracy work. Abdicating fundamental policy decisions to the courts does not make for democracy, rule by the people. It makes for rule by an elite, an elite which has been called the "aristocracy of the robe." They may have gained their positions by succeeding at Harvard or Yale law schools and in the arcana of legal academia rather than through their parentage, but an aristocracy they are nonetheless.

### *The Missing Check and Balance*

Besides negating democratic government, allowing the Supreme Court to exercise essentially exclusive power over changing the meaning of our Constitution is deeply problematic in other ways. At the core of our constitutional system is the notion of checks and balances. In one of his most famous passages from *The Federalist*, Madison wrote that "if men were angels, no government would be necessary." However, "in framing a government which is to be administered by men over men, the great difficulty lies in this: you must first enable the government to control the governed; and in the next place oblige it to control itself." How do you get the government to "control itself"? The framers' solution, Madison continued, was to set up the "distribution of the supreme powers of the State" so as "to divide and arrange the several offices so that each may be a check on the other -- that the private interest of every individual may be a sentinel over the public rights."

Although it is not explicitly authorized by the Constitution, the idea of judicial review, that the Supreme Court can rule that one of Congress' laws violates the Constitution, fits nicely into the idea of checks and balances. The problem is that, while judicial review allows the Supreme Court to force Congress to follow the Constitution, nothing forces the Supreme Court to follow the Constitution! As noted above, the modern legal elite's answer is that the Supreme Court polices itself, but that is not how constitutional checks and balances are supposed to work.

Theoretically, there are checks on the Supreme Court in the Constitution. These are supposed to be the President's power to nominate and the Senate's to approve Supreme Court justices (and other federal judges). If we accept that the Supreme Court can at any time overturn any act of the elected branches, this one-time check only at the time of nomination seems a very small check indeed. Members of the democratically elected branches pass on a Supreme Court justice but once, yet that justice, together with only four colleagues, can void the other branches' actions an unlimited number of times throughout a life tenure which is limited only by health and death.

This enormous imbalance between the one time that elected federal officeholders can check a Supreme Court justice as compared to the unlimited number of times that justice can overrule the democratic branches of government has also turned Supreme Court nominations into furious partisan brawls. For example, recall the year-long battle between President Obama and the Republican Senate over replacing the late Justice Antonin Scalia. The passion these nominations stir is directly related to the ever-increasing power of that position. As progressive writer Ezra Klein explained at the time of Elena Kagan's nomination, "we're talking about a lifetime appointment to a body with vast power and almost unlimited jurisdiction."

## *Vast Unlimited Power: for the Judges or the People?*

Vast and almost unlimited power. The Supreme Court of the United States is certainly not the only governing body in the world, or in history, to claim vast power over almost every subject. In fact, Americans lived under such a government in 1776, and had some objections to it. When some of those Americans met in Philadelphia over the hot summer of 1787 to set out a plan for a national government, their goal was to create a government system where the parts would check and balance each other so that no one part would have "vast power and almost unlimited jurisdiction." Something has gotten seriously out of kilter in the 235 years since then.

Although they differ on reasons and remedies, both progressives and conservatives today agree that our national government does not represent the American people. As originally framed, the Constitution's amendment power was to be the People's ultimate check on the excesses of the Supreme Court and the rest of our national government. However, the constitutional amendment process now is dead for all practical purposes.

Could an alliance, even if temporary, of sincere progressives and conservatives revive the People's amendment power? The Amendment Amendment proposed here hopes to accomplish this by being acceptable to both. Its provisions are designed to balance the objectives of both progressives and conservatives. It is not the revision of the amendment process which an all-progressive group would draft, nor is it what an all-conservative group would write. Instead, it tries to combine features which would be favored by one side and yet tolerable to the other. It is therefore no one's perfect solution. However, it might, just might, return control of our national Constitution and government to the American people.

The Amendment Amendment would reform Article Five with procedures which would permit the people and their states to initiate constitutional change. It would permit the people in their states to decide the great questions of constitutional interpretation. It is only a bit longer than the current Article Five. Each of the provisions is there for a purpose, based on our history of experience with Article Five over the last two and a third centuries. Of course, Congress would still pass laws, and the courts would fill in the little interstices where it is not quite clear how the language applies. But with a renewed power of amendment, the ultimate say would be with the People in their states, not the power elites in Washington, DC or their cohorts on Wall Street and K Street, and in the mainstream media.

### The Most Difficult in the World

The American Constitution is the oldest written constitution in the world. In its time, the idea that it could be amended was an innovation. Previously, written fundamental laws were holy writ, never to be altered. Since our Constitution went into operation in 1789 many other constitutions have been written. In fact, there are only six nations in the world which do not have one. All 50 states have constitutions as well. Political scientist Donald Lutz has compared the amendment provisions of many of these constitutions by looking quantitatively at how often amendment occurs with various requirements. He then created a scale to compare what we might call "amendability." His conclusion is that the United States Constitution is by far the most difficult in the world to amend.

For example, while about half of our states' constitutions require a two-thirds vote of the state legislature to start an amendment of the state constitution, the rest require less than two-thirds vote of the legislature. Some do require that these votes occur in consecutive legislative sessions. After the state legislature approves an amendment, many states do require that the proposal also be approved by a ballot measure, but that is only a majority vote. None require a three-fourths vote of anything or anyone after the state legislature has acted. Thus, none are as difficult to amend as the federal constitution under Article Five, which requires two-thirds vote of Congress and then approval by three fourths of the states on top of that.

A similar picture emerges when one looks at other democratic nations. Of particular interest are other federal democracies. In Canada amendments need only be proposed by simple majorities in both houses of parliament, and then approved by just two thirds of the provinces (but the approving provinces must have at least half the nation's population). In Australia a simple majority in both houses of parliament is also sufficient, and then an amendment is submitted to a national referendum where a simple majority also suffices, although the referendum approval must be by simple majorities in a majority of the states as well. Similarly, in Switzerland proposals passed by a majority of the legislature then only have to pass a referendum by simple majorities in a majority of the cantons. The Swiss do have a major democratic feature in that amendment proposals may also be initiated by popular vote. In Germany two-thirds votes in both houses of the national legislature are alone sufficient to amend Germany's constitution, or Basic Law. (However, the upper house is elected directly by the state legislatures, like in the United States before the 17th Amendment, so effectively two thirds of the *Länder* also approve the amendment.) Again, no other federal democracy has double thresholds as steep as Article Five's two-thirds/three-fourths.

Lutz notes that the result of these high thresholds is not constitutional stability.  Instead, in the United States constitutional change comes through judicial action.  In an analysis of "the way in which the Constitution in practice changes," University of Chicago law professor David Strauss has written that "formal amendments are a sidelight.  The living Constitution, that is the evolution of precedents and traditions [in the courts], is the real show."

# THREE

## Making the People the 'Real Show':
## How the Amendment Amendment Would Work

The Amendment Amendment will move the "real show" back to the People, where it belongs. Here is how the Amendment Amendment achieves that. (It may be helpful to refer to the actual text set out in the Appendix):

*Eliminate the convention requirement and let the states launch amendment proposals directly.* As noted earlier, the current Article Five has an unused provision for two thirds of the states to call a convention to propose amendments. For reasons which will be discussed later, this convention method has never been used, and never will be. The whole convention idea was an unfortunate last minute addition to the Constitution over James Madison's very wise objections that it would be an unworkable procedural mess. However, even if they didn't get the procedure right, the framers all agreed that the states should be able to initiate amendment proposals independent of Congress.

If there is no convention, how would amendment proposals by the states be launched? One solution is to let any state vote for an amendment and send it to the other states for approval. However, this runs two risks. First, a single state might vote for idiosyncratic proposals dreamed up by one influential state legislator. These perhaps oddball proposals could crowd attention away from more serious proposals. Second, different proposals with the same objective might be started by different states. For example, there are many different versions of amendments to overturn *Citizens United* or to require a balanced federal budget. Different proposals from different states would be counter-productive, dividing the efforts of those who are in basic agreement on the objectives of the amendment proposals.

Another possibility is the proposal from the 1787 convention that two thirds of the states be required to initiate an amendment proposal. That may have been manageable when that meant eight states (there were 12 at the convention), but 34 states is quite a different matter logistically. And it could take a long time to get to 34 states, which leaves more time for conflicting proposals with the same objective to get started.

Therefore, the Amendment Amendment proposes that five states are required to launch an amendment proposal, acting within a four-month period. This will screen out the idiosyncratic proposals of a single state, and encourage amendment proponents to agree on a single text. It will be much less likely that there will be two different proposals on the same subject when that would mean starting them in ten different states rather than two different states. The four-month window is to allow enough time for state legislative sessions to overlap. Finally, only requiring five states to get started will facilitate proposals from groups without a lot of resources at the beginning, so that the amendment process is not exclusively the preserve of groups with the funding to reach 34 states right away.

Probably the only reason anyone thought of using the convention method at all was because in 1787 it could take weeks for one exchange of correspondence between different parts of the country. Today modern travel and communications technologies make a face-to-face meeting to work out language unnecessary. Of course, in-person talks can be useful, and states could still get together to discuss amendment proposals. Meetings of the National Conference of State Legislatures, a bipartisan organization whose membership is all 50 states' legislatures, could provide a convenient locale for such discussions. But, unlike an Article Five convention, these would be advisory only. Amendment proposals could only be officially launched by state legislatures.

*The approval thresholds are lowered, slightly.*  As noted above, the United States Constitution is by far the most difficult in the world to amend.   (The difficulty of reaching the two-thirds vote required in Congress was dramatically portrayed in the movie *Lincoln* about the Thirteenth Amendment abolishing slavery.)    Therefore, the Amendment Amendment slightly reduces Article Five's current two-thirds/three-fourths thresholds.   If an amendment does not receive approval in Congress, two thirds of the states are required to approve it instead of three fourths (that is 34 states of 50 instead of 38). However, if Congress approves the amendment, then only five eighths of the states are required to ratify it for it to become effective (32 states out of 50).   By giving amendment proposals a "bonus" of requiring fewer state approvals if they also pass Congress we help avoid swinging to the opposite extreme of completely excluding Congress from the amendment process.   In Congress the amendment process is also facilitated by reducing the required vote from two thirds to five eighths (62.5% versus 66 $2/3$%).

You may wonder why the Amendment Amendment is not bolder in lowering the requirements to, say, three–fifths vote in Congress and of the states for ratification.  The reason is because the Amendment Amendment is actually not very bold.  Indeed, as noted in Chapter One, the Amendment Amendement's thresholds are actually statistically equivalent to the original thresholds set when the Nation was much smaller, with far fewer actors needed for amendment.  Five eighths is 62.5%, essentially the same as the 62% yielded by the probability analysis discussed in Chapter One.

Amending the Constitution is serious business.  By lowering the new thresholds to what are basically only "one step" lower than the existing thresholds, we are moving very carefully.  Allowing states to initiate amendment proposals will facilitate much more amendment activity in any case.  After some experience with the new level of popular participation in the amending process, we can revisit the thresholds. If it appears that the new thresholds are still too high, they can be further revised using the Amendment Amendment's own procedures.

The Amendment Amendment adds one more provision to the thresholds. If two thirds of the states approve an amendment without approval by Congress, those states must have at least a majority of the nation's population. Although it has never happened, and as a practical matter is quite impossible, this does eliminate the purely theoretical possibility that states with less than a majority of the nation's population might amend the Constitution. (As of the 2020 census, the 34 least populous states have 30% of the nation's population.) As we saw, Canada, where there are big population differences among the provinces as there are among our states, uses this requirement to balance respect for the autonomy of its provinces against the need to assure that a national majority supports a constitutional amendment.

*Referenda may be used to approve an amendment.* Article Five now provides that amendments are to be ratified "by the Legislatures of three fourths of the several States, or by Conventions in three fourths thereof, as … proposed by the Congress." In 1918 the Ohio legislature ratified the 18th Amendment establishing national prohibition on the "manufacture, sale or transportation of intoxicating liquors." This ratification was communicated to the U. S. Secretary of State and the amendment was declared effective. However, in the meantime, in accordance with Ohio law a petition for a referendum on the ratification was successful. In the subsequent referendum the decision of the legislature was reversed. In 1920, in *Hawke v. Smith* the Supreme Court rejected the Ohio referendum action and upheld the ratification of the 18th Amendment on the grounds that Article Five speaks of action by a "Legislature," which term, the Court declared, did not include popular referenda.

Referenda were generally unknown at the time the Constitution was written. However, since then they have become widely used in connection with constitutional amendments. Most of our states use them, as do other federal democracies like Canada, Australia and Switzerland. And the idea of a referendum is actually not as foreign to Article Five as *Hawke* would make it seem. Article Five currently provides that Congress may decide that amendments be ratified by state conventions rather than the legislatures. This has only happened once. Ironically, it was for the 21$^{st}$ Amendment, which repealed the prohibition of liquor mandated by the 18$^{th}$ Amendment which was the subject of the *Hawke* case. With the 21$^{st}$ Amendment, the state conventions effectively operated as referenda since almost all states required candidates to the conventions to declare their position in advance. The conventions merely ratified the popular vote. Indeed, the New Hampshire convention completed its ratification of the 21$^{st}$ Amendment and adjourned in 17 minutes flat. Approving constitutional amendments by referenda is thus in practice not materially different than the state convention ratification mode already authorized by the current Article Five.

Therefore, the Amendment Amendment allows a state to use a ballot referendum to approve a constitutional amendment instead of having the state legislature vote on it. However, the decision is left up to the state legislatures, so this does not interfere in their right to be primary players in this important matter. Different states will probably take different approaches. Some may leave the decision in the hands of the legislature. Sometimes the legislature may nonetheless vote to put a specific amendment proposal on the ballot. And some states may choose to pass a law or state constitutional amendment requiring that all federal constitutional amendments be submitted to ballot approval. Which approach is used will depend on each state's traditions and the will of its people.

Although not a part of the formal Amendment Amendment proposal, there is another possible use for a referendum. The Amendment Amendment reduces the numerical requirement for state approvals from three fourths of the states to five eighths of the states if Congress also approves the amendment. However, what about a situation where five eighths of the states have approved an amendment but Congress still balks? In this case, we might consider a one-time national referendum. To make such a referendum comparable to a congressional approval, it should require the same five-eighths supermajority (62.5%). Such a procedure could also provide for the first time an opportunity for the United States to experiment with a nationwide referendum, a procedure which is common in many other democratic nations. However, in the interest of streamlining an already quite comprehensive proposal, this provision has been left out of the Amendment Amendment in the Appendix at the end of this book.

*States may rescind prior amendment approvals.* Article Five does not say whether states may rescind a previous amendment ratification. The question first arose in the very convoluted context of the ratifications of the 14th and 15th Amendments after the Civil War in 1868 and 1870, respectively. In both cases southern states which had previously ratified the amendments purported to rescind their ratifications, but their rescission attempts were ignored by Congress. On the other hand, in both cases a last minute ratification by another state (which happened to be Georgia for both) meant that the amendments would nevertheless have met the three-fourths state ratification requirement and been effective even with the rescissions.

The issue of rescission came up again in the struggle to ratify the Equal Rights Amendment in the 1970s, when several states voted to rescind their previous ratifications. Ultimately the ERA never achieved the necessary 38 state ratifications even counting those of the rescinding states. However, the contest did produce a controversial federal district court decision in favor of rescission, which the Supreme

Court never reviewed because the passage of the ratification deadline rendered it moot.

Legal writers' arguments as to whether a state can rescind a prior amendment ratification generally seem to correspond with whether the writer likes or dislikes the proposed amendment in question. However, these technical arguments are irrelevant when dealing with a constitutional amendment because it will sweep away any technicalities based on the previous Article Five. There remain three policy arguments in favor and one against allowing rescission. The one against is that allowing rescission could make it confusing to determine the status of an amendment's approval. The best response to this came from the distinguished constitutional scholar Charles Black, who reportedly quipped that "anyone who can't count to thirty-eight ought to be in a less complicated line of work."

The arguments for allowing rescission are more substantial. It is broadly agreed that a state which has rejected an amendment proposal may later change its mind and approve it. Would not simple fairness then require that the reverse should also be allowed? Another point which is broadly accepted is that the approval of constitutional amendments should be reasonably contemporaneous. It really would be confusing if we had many repeats of the 27th Amendment, which was first proposed in 1791 and only finally ratified over two centuries later in 1992. Allowing states to rescind a prior approval assures that there really is agreement on the amendment at the time when the state ratification threshold is met.

Third, allowing rescission opens the possibility that the people may speak on an amendment in a subsequent election either by specific referendum, such as in Ohio with the 18th Amendment which led to the *Hawke* case, or by voting for or against state legislators based on their vote on the amendment. This also enhances the possibilities for deliberation on a proposed amendment. For all these reasons the

Amendment Amendment explicitly allows for rescission of previous approvals except immediately prior to final effectiveness.

*Set expirations also assure contemporaneous consensus.* The Amendment Amendment also seeks to promote contemporaneous approval of an amendment by setting fixed time limits for an amendment to be approved. Setting time limits also clears the calendar of amendment proposals which are failing to capture sufficient acceptance so that other proposals can come forward. Since the early 1900s Congress has been setting a time limit of seven years for amendments to be approved, so the Amendment Amendment formally adopts that time limit for amendments initiated by Congress. A slightly longer nine-year time limit is set for amendment proposals initiated by states since it may require more organization to promote a proposal among many states. Obviously, this will lead amendment proponents to favor state initiation but, as we have seen, Congress has not been using its right to initiate amendments much anyway.

*Other clarifications.* The earliest Supreme Court case involving Article Five was *Hollingsworth v. Virginia* in 1798. In *Hollingsworth* the Supreme Court decided that an amendment did not have to have the President's signature. Since then, it has been assumed that amendment was strictly a legislative function, not subject the approval or veto of an executive such as the President or a state governor. However, it has never been certain that this is true in all cases. Therefore, the Amendment Amendment makes it explicit that action by government executive officers is not applicable to the amendment process except for conducting referenda. Other Supreme Court cases have suggested that only Congress can make the rules for constitutional amendments. However, these are vague rulings, of uncertain applicability other than the specific circumstances of those cases. Since the Amendment Amendment strives to increase the states' role in constitutional amendment, it overrides these cases and allows each state to make its own rules governing the approval of constitutional amendments.

# FOUR

## Why Keep State Equality in Ratification?

Perhaps the biggest issue in reforming Article Five is voting. The current Article Five uses state equality, where each state's approval counts the same as every other state's approval despite different population sizes. The Amendment Amendment preserves the use of state equality, with the addition of a requirement similar to Canada's that when two thirds of the states ratify an amendment without congressional approval the ratifying states must have at least half of the nation's population. However, the states' populations vary significantly. Why should California and Vermont be equal? Shouldn't everyone's vote count the same?

In order to understand why it is important to keep voting by states despite different populations, we must look at the underlying structure of the American constitutional system. The genius of the system created by the 1787 Constitution is its balancing of competing powers in order to preserve liberty. It tried to create a balance (since upset by the rise of the Supreme Court to primacy) between the branches of the federal government by providing that each had some sort of control or check on the other. Thus, for example, only Congress can pass laws but the President must sign them.

The counter-balancing of the federal and state governments is another one of these fundamental structural protections. In another of Madison's famous passages from *The Federalist*, he wrote that the "powers delegated by the proposed Constitution to the federal government are few and defined. Those which are to remain in the State governments are numerous and indefinite." There has been a continuing centralization of power in the national government over the last century, and a concomitant decrease in local autonomy and

34

individual freedom. A major goal of the Amendment Amendment is to answer George Mason, to restore some of that federal-state balance by reinvigorating a check on the national government's potential to dominate the rights and liberties of individual citizens and their state governments. The states are a critical element of this process, because they can act institutionally and constitutionally to offset federal power in ways that individual citizens can not. Preserving state equality in the amendment process empowers the states as constitutional entities to serve this end.

Even if there are reasons for a strong national government, it comes at a high cost, for the federal government in Washington is unavoidably remote from the people, certainly more remote than state governments. It is simply a matter of arithmetic. The 435 members of the national House of Representatives have on average more than 700,000 constituents in each of their districts. In contrast, the more than 7,000 state legislators represent on average just over 50,000 constituents each, not to mention their greater geographical proximity to their constituents. For the vast majority of Americans, their state capital is much closer than Washington, DC.

Preserving voting by states will also facilitate participation by grassroots organizations. The most commonly proposed alternative, a single national referendum, would limit participation to those who have the resources to fund a nation-wide campaign. In contrast, it will be much easier for causes without big money backing to progress if they only have to move state by state.

Even for those who do not appreciate the value of preserving states as a strong counter-balance to the power of the national government, there is a practical counter-argument. Preserving state equality will actually make no difference in the outcome of any amendment proposal.

### *State Equality Will Yield the Same Outcomes as a National Vote*

Historically no amendment has ever been enacted by states representing a minority of the nation's population. Indeed, ratifying states have always represented substantial majorities of the nation's population, *and this will certainly continue to be the case.* To understand why, we must examine the distribution of more and less populous states. It has always been true that the less populous states have less than a majority of the nation's population. However, a more complex picture emerges when one looks more closely at the data. For example, over the sixty-year period between the 1960 and 2020 censuses, the 34 least populous states stayed consistently at about a third of the total national population, and the 16 most populous at about two thirds. However, which states constituted the 16 most populous changed significantly. Missouri and Wisconsin dropped out of the group of the 16 most populous states and into the group of 34 less populous states, to be replaced by Washington and Arizona.

Also, more and less populous states are found in all regions of the nation. New York, the fourth most populous state, adjoins Vermont and Connecticut, respectively the 49th and 29th most populous states. Texas, the second most populous state, adjoins states ranked 25th (Louisiana), 33rd (Arkansas), 28th (Oklahoma), and 36th (New Mexico). The most populous state, California, shares its longest border with Nevada, the 32nd most populous state.

More important than this geographical distribution of more and less populous states is their ideological distribution. The theoretical argument against state equality is that the 34 least populous states might join to pass a constitutional amendment adverse to the interests of the citizens of the 16 most populous states. We might call this the "OK-VT conspiracy" hypothesis. It assumes that the legislature of Oklahoma, which is four fifths Republican as of the most recent election, and that of Vermont, which is three quarters Democrat and

Progressive, would collude on some constitutional issue on which their neighbors Texas and New York would be joined in opposition. In fact, more and less populated states span the ideological spectrum. An alliance of all the less populous states against all of the more populous states is inconceivable as a practical matter in the real-world United States as it actually exists.

Those who worry about a combination of less populous states against the more populous states base their views on the perception that less populous states are rural and conservative whereas more populous states are urban and liberal. However, this is an egregious oversimplification. It certainly does not describe less populous liberal states such as Hawaii (40th), Rhode Island (44th), Delaware (45th) or Vermont (49th) or more populous conservative or conservative-leaning states such as Texas (2nd), Florida (3rd), Georgia (8th) or North Carolina (9th). It ignores such complexities as the high degree of urbanization of many less populous states, including many traditionally conservative states. An example of the complex reality of our nation can be seen by noting that Vermont, one of the most consistently liberal states, is also the most rural state in the nation whereas Utah, one of the most consistently conservative states, is also one of the most urbanized (89% of its population lives in urban areas compared to the national average of 79%) The perception also fails to take into account the complex internal political complexions of states both populous and less populous such as Ohio (7th) or Iowa (31st).

We can actually demonstrate the broad ideological range among more and less populous states by using Congress as a proxy. The Senate is apportioned by state equality and the House of Representatives by population. Each state has two Senators no matter what its population, which is comparable to giving each state one vote in approving constitutional amendments. On the other hand, the allocation of seats in the House of Representatives is based on population. For example, California has 52 Representatives and

Vermont has only one. Thus, voting in the House of Representatives is generally comparable to approving a constitutional amendment on some basis that tracks the total national population.

Since 1947 the Americans for Democratic Action (ADA), a liberal political advocacy organization, has scored the voting records of all members of Congress. Political scientists Tim Groseclose, Steven Levitt, and James Snyder analyzed the ADA voting record scores from 1947 through 1996. This analysis was carried forward through 2006 in a study by Sarah Anderson and Philip Habel. These analyses show that the liberal/conservative scores over that 60 year time period for both the House and the Senate have not differed significantly. In other words, over a sixty-year period there has not been any consistent ideological difference in voting based on state equality (the Senate) and population (the House of Representatives).

Of course, the scores have not always been identical at every point in time. Due to the different term lengths of the House and Senate (two years versus six years), the composition of the Senate shifts more slowly. There have been times when the Senate was more conservative than the House, such as in the 1950s and 1980s, but it was also generally more liberal than the House in the 1960s and 1970s. Looking at overall trends the political scientists found the Senate slightly more conservative over the entire period. However, on the other hand, the ADA's own analysis of its own data reached the opposite generalization, that the Senate overall has been slightly more liberal than the House over the same period. In either case, the difference has been small.

What differences there have been between the Senate and House scores have never been large (at most five points on a 60-point scale) and the gap usually has closed within a few election cycles. Further, even when there were these small gaps, the trends of the two chambers' scores in more liberal or more conservative directions have generally tracked each other until they rejoined.

The ADA has not updated its comparison of the House and Senate, but its conservative counterpart, the American Conservative Union (ACU), also tracks the voting records of all members of Congress. Its comparison of the entire House and entire Senate also shows little variation between the two chambers from the 1980s to the present, generally a point or two on a 100 point scale. Despite the vastly different ways in which seats in the two chambers are allocated, and despite shifting control of the chambers between the two political parties, the ACU found that the two chambers have had close to the same aggregate degree of conservatism over the past five decades including through to the present time.

This ideological comparison of more and less populous states provided by looking at the long-term voting records of the Senate and the House of Representatives strongly suggests that the outcome of enacting an amendment by a system which preserves state equality would not differ from one using some kind of national vote. Although national voting has a theoretical appeal, it will make little difference in practice if we preserve elements of state equality as a political compromise in order to achieve a reformed Article Five. Federalism is very important to conservatives, so such a compromise is needed to bring together the progressive/conservative political coalition which is essential to get any reform of Article Five through Congress.

Finally, there is an overriding practical consideration for preserving a system of state equality in a reformed amendment process. Any reform of Article Five must pass through the procedures of the current Article Five, which means the approval of two thirds of the U.S. Senate, and then ratification by three fourths of the states, including less populated states. It is politically unrealistic to think that U. S. Senators and state legislators from less populous states will accept amendment only by national population without regard for the status of the states. They will insist that any reform of Article Five continue to guarantee that their constituents retain some of the structure protecting them from domination by larger states which their predecessors fought so hard to assure at the convention of 1787. The Amendment Amendment offers such an accommodation.

Comparisons of "liberal quotient" over a 60 year period (1946 – 2007), as calculated by the Americans for Democratic Action. Over that period in both parties there was no significant ideological difference between the Senate (with seats allocated by state equality) and the House of Representatives (with seats allocated by population):

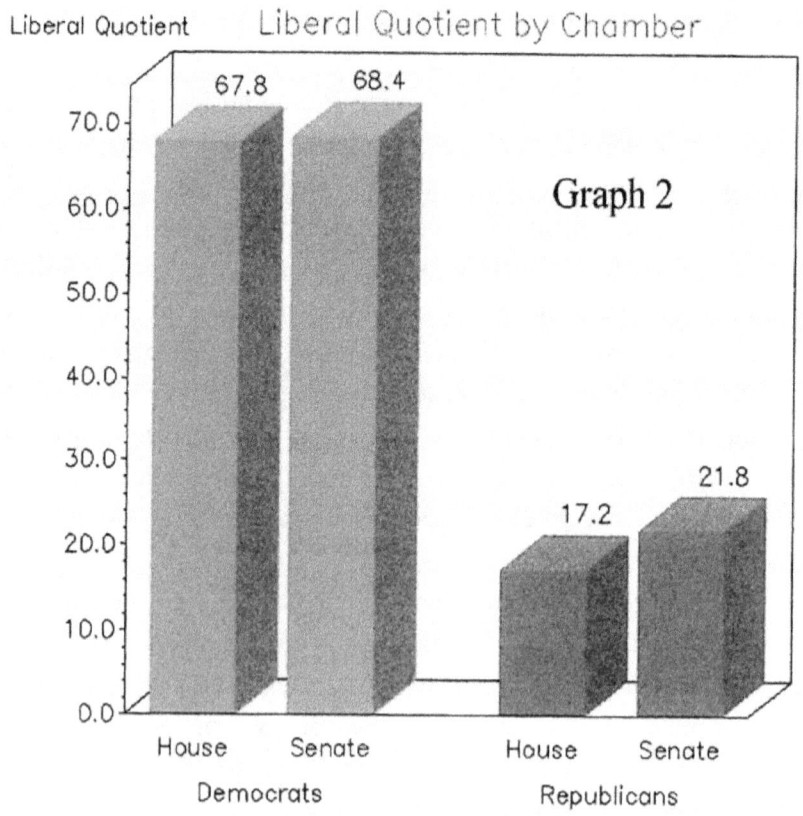

*© Americans for Democratic Action. Used with permission.*

# FIVE

## Why Not Call an Article Five Convention?

A last objection to the Amendment Amendment is this: we already have a method in the current Article Five for initiation of amendments by the states. Why not just have two thirds of the states call a new constitutional convention?

The last weekend of September 2011 in Cambridge, Massachusetts was warm, presaging what would be a mild winter. However, a far more peculiar warmth was to be found that weekend in some of the halls of the Harvard Law School. A conference was convened, not an unusual occurrence at an academic institution. But this conference was not your typical academic conclave. The Conference on the Constitutional Convention (ConConCon for short) did not feature any arcane academic papers, and most of its attendees had probably not been inside a classroom in a long time.

Equally atypical were its co-sponsors. These were a progressive campaign finance reform organization called Fix Congress First, and the Tea Party Patriots, one of the leading Tea Party umbrella organizations. Activists making plans to travel to Occupy Washington mingled with activists looking to repeal the 16th Amendment authorizing the federal income tax. Yet the atmosphere was positively convivial. The progressives and Occupiers seemed pleasantly surprised at how little the Tea Partiers frothed at the mouth, and the Tea Partiers grew increasingly comfortable that they were not at risk of arrest on suspicion of racism by Harvard PC speech code patrols.

Much of the conviviality came from a shared common ground. Article Five provides that two thirds of the states may request that Congress call a convention "for proposing amendments." As noted, this method has never been used, and is thus even more moribund

41

than having Congress initiate amendments by two-thirds vote. However, the convention method has stirred from time to time (Lincoln referenced it in the quote from his first inaugural at the beginning of this book), and it is stirring again.

At least that September weekend, the ConConCon was probably the largest gathering in America of people who even knew that Article Five provides the possibility of calling a convention to propose amendments to the Constitution. All were looking for a way to revive the amendment process because they believed that the Constitution needs amending.

What those amendments would be varied, to say the least. Some attendees circulated texts of a constitution for a Socialist Republic of America, but even the Occupy sympathizers saw them as cranks. Most progressives wanted to amend the Constitution to reverse the *Citizens United* decision. Harvard law professor Lawrence Lessig, the conference co-chair from the progressive side, had just published a book called *Republic, Lost: How Money Corrupts Congress – And a Plan to Stop It*. His ultimate plan to stop it is to call a constitutional convention under Article Five to propose amendments to prevent money from influencing politicians. He was echoed by a parade of activists from many different progressive organizations fighting that good fight.

However, the progressives were hardly limited to that plan. One of the presenters was the distinguished University of Texas law professor Sanford Levinson. His book is called *Our Undemocratic Constitution: Where the Constitution Goes Wrong (And How We the People Can Correct It)*. Professor Levinson's proposals include abolishing the Senate, the presidential veto, the Electoral College, recess appointments, life tenure for Supreme Court justices, and the age and residence qualifications for office. He would also allow the Congress to remove a President for any reason by a two-thirds vote. Progressive academics like Lessig and Levinson dream of an open-ended constitutional convention which could engage in a "national conversation" about many reforms to our system of government.

The conservative attendees were less ambitious. The only specific amendment proposal advanced by the Tea Partiers was the National Debt Relief Amendment. An alternative to the better known balanced budget amendment, it would require consent of a majority of the states to increase the federal debt. One of its major proponents, a North Dakota state senator named Curtis Olafson, announced that his state and Louisiana had both passed resolutions requesting Congress to call a constitutional convention to approve it. He was supported by a delegation from the Goldwater Institute, a prominent conservative/libertarian think tank based in Phoenix, Arizona.

A few attendees did not care what amendments an Article Five convention might propose. They just wanted there to be a convention. Most prominent of these was Bill Walker, a founder and guiding light of group called Friends of Article Five. A sixtyish bull of a man from Seattle, Walker is a classic American eccentric who has committed his life to the goal of making an Article Five convention happen. Walker and his group claim that there have been more than 700 state applications to Congress to convene such a convention. Other scholars put the count at closer to 400. In either case, the number is well in excess of the 34 states required by Article Five. Walker has brought two lawsuits to have the courts force the Congress to call a convention. Both have been dismissed on the grounds that calling a convention is strictly a congressional responsibility with which the courts can not interfere.

At the ConConCon Walker announced that a federal criminal complaint had just been filed accusing the members of Congress of breaching their oaths of office for failure to call the convention. According to Walker's website, the complaint has since been buried by the Justice Department. However, at the time Walker seemed to feel that this was going to be the turning point in his life's work. With a solemn, almost valedictory, air he told the assemblage that he had accomplished his mission, and that it was now up to those assembled to carry on the task of realizing the second constitutional convention.

Of course, if you have not heard about this impending momentous event, it is probably because the Justice Department is no more likely to force Congress to call a constitutional convention than the judges in Walker's lawsuits. To the extent that anyone in Congress pays even the slightest passing attention to the matter, they dismiss the 400 or 700 state applications because of one of the numerous fundamental problems with the convention method of amending the Constitution. This is whether the subject matter of the convention can be limited. The overwhelming majority of the state convention calls relate to some specific purpose. If one state calls for a constitutional convention to pass a balanced budget amendment and another calls for one to allow states to proportion their legislatures on a basis other than population (the two subjects which have generated the most applications in the last fifty years), can you aggregate the two in counting up the applications from 34 states required for a convention? Congress apparently thinks not.

At the ConConCon it was also apparent that this issue is a fundamental divide even among the pro-convention forces. The progressives were undisturbed by, even preferred, an open-ended general convention. For the conservatives an unlimited convention was unthinkable. This was made clear by Mark Meckler, a co-founder of the Tea Party Patriots and the conservative co-chair of the conference, in his closing remarks. He hated to throw water on the wonderful kumbaya spirit of the gathering Meckler said, "but no conservative state legislator is ever going support a call for an unlimited convention."[4]

### *Liberal vs. Liberal, Conservative vs. Conservative*

Amongst the devotees of Article Five, the debate over whether an Article Five convention could be limited as to its subject matter has raged on and off since the 1960s. Many fear that a general open-ended convention would "run away" like the original convention of 1787, proposing schemes far beyond what was contemplated by the participating states. While convention advocates dispute that interpretation, it is hard to dispute that many state legislators and others in 1787 thought the convention at Philadelphia that summer was just going to revise the Articles of Confederation which had governed the United States since the Revolutionary War. They further assumed that the changes were to be subject to unanimous approval by the states as provided by the Articles of Confederation. Many Americans of the time were thus shocked when an entirely new scheme of government emerged from the closed meetings of that first convention, and one which proclaimed itself effective upon the approval of only nine states.

Even though the 1787 Constitution has endured for over two centuries, and itself provides for the summoning of an amending convention, the boldness of the 1787 convention hangs over the prospects for a second convention. In vain limited convention advocates point out that, even if a convention produced cockamamie amendment proposals, they would still have to be approved by three fourths of the states. The whole convention idea is just too uncertain. Politicians do not advance by upsetting the status quo, be it liberal or

---

[4] Meckler has since left the Tea Party Patriots and is now leading a drive to call an exclusively conservative Article Five convention to initiate amendments limited to reducing the powers of the federal government.

conservative, and nothing would threaten the political status quo like a runaway constitutional convention. Any legislator who voted to call such a convention would be held accountable for whatever it produced, and politicians do not even like to be held accountable for things they can control, let alone a wild untried proposal like this.

The world of convention opponents is not limited to the state legislators who have repeatedly stopped at the brink of issuing a final convention call. (Most recently, in the 1980s 32 of the necessary 34 states called for a convention to pass a balanced budget amendment. Instead Congress passed the largely ineffectual and useless Gramm-Rudman-Hollings Act.) While the ConConCon attracted a few hundred progressive convention supporters, in his book Professor Levinson laments that fear of a new constitutional convention is "more likely present in persons who identify themselves as 'liberals' than among 'conservatives.' Most liberals these days appear to be … terrified of the passions of their fellow citizens." Even Levinson "unhappily acknowledges … the potential for disaster in certain kinds of pseudo-democratic, demagogic politics from which the United States is certainly not immune."

While Levinson is willing to take the risk in order to try for a more democratic Constitution, many other progressives are not. They see a constitutional convention as opening the path to possibly subtle infringements on basic constitutional liberties. No one thinks that such a convention would propose to repeal the Bill of Rights outright. But it is not beyond possibility that "exceptions" and "clarifications" would be proposed which could erode fundamental freedoms and open the path to future deteriorations beyond the already advanced infringements allowed for such exceptions as national security.

Theodore Sorenson, author and long-time Democratic Party figure, warned that "no one can safely assume that the delegates to such a Convention, once seated and in action, would wish to go home

46

without trying their hand at improving many parts of the delicately balanced document. All of us know of the pressures that will then build up to amend the Bill of Rights. ... Whatever one's party or philosophy, whatever his position on a particular amendment or his faith on our State legislative bodies, the prospect of wide-open dabbling with the classic work ... can only fill the constitutionalist with alarm." At the time of the push for a convention to initiate a balanced budget amendment in the late 1970s, President Jimmy Carter feared that it "might result in unlimited amendments which could change the basic thrust, the philosophy and the structure of our government" and Vice President Walter Mondale called it "the worst idea I ever heard."

If progressives are divided among themselves on the question of calling a second constitutional convention, conservatives are at war. Some conservatives have long promoted the calling of an Article Five convention. Swinging the balance of power back to the states from the federal government is a fundamental plank of modern conservatism. And yet, despite this argument, many conservative states in recent years have passed resolutions specifically rescinding all of their previous convention applications. This is probably largely due to the efforts of two important conservative organizations which most people under the age of 50 have probably never heard of. The John Birch Society and Phyllis Schlafly's Eagle Forum have made opposition to calls for a convention among their primary missions. The John Birch Society is a controversial anti-Communist organization begun in the 1950s, and best known for its charge that Dwight Eisenhower was pro-Communist. Opposition to an Article Five convention is so important to them that the Birch Society must have had a mole at the ConConCon, for within hours of the end of the conference their website was happily announcing that the progressives had "failed" to convince the Tea Partiers to support a constitutional convention.

Phyllis Schlafly's renown came from her almost single-handed success in stopping the Equal Rights Amendment in the late 1970s and

47

early 1980s. Although ignored thereafter by the mainstream media, she went on to become a *grande dame* of the right. She re-emerged as a controversial national figure when she became one of the most vocal conservative supporters of Donald Trump. Schlafly seems to have picked up an aversion to amendment in general from her fight against the ERA.

Although calling an Article Five convention was not an issue in the 2016 or other recent elections, Schlafly devoted an entire chapter in her last book, *The Conservative Case for Trump* (published posthumously as she passed away in September 2016) to opposing such a convention. There, she warned, "Democrats would propose constitutional amendments to ensure socialized heath care, or 'free' higher education for everyone, or enshrining gay marriage into the Constitution." Earlier she had warned that George Soros funded organizations would control the convention with the mainstream media promoting the participants favored by Soros and Barack Obama. She evoked the chaotic pro-union demonstrations in Madison, Wisconsin as a foreshadowing of what an Article Five convention would be like.

For a long time another very influential conservative anti-convention figure was talk show host Mark Levin. The subtitle of his bestselling book *Men in Black: How the Supreme Court Is Destroying America* neatly sums up Levin's opinion of amendment by litigation and judicial review. Yet, he was dubious about an Article Five convention. For example, at a speech at the Ronald Reagan Library he warned of "what a freak show convention that would be. ... A runaway convention would be a runaway country. I'm just not comfortable with it. As a young man I wrote Barry Goldwater a letter and said 'what about this convention' and he said 'hell no to convention, I can't imagine that any group of Americans today can do better than they [the founders] did.'"

However, Levin has changed his view. In his book *The Liberty Amendments: Restoring the American Republic*, he proposes a series of constitutional amendments to put America back on its original constitutional track. In the book, which debuted at the top of the bestseller lists, Levin backed the call of an Article Five convention to initiate his amendment program. Interestingly, one of his amendment proposals is to allow two thirds of the states to amend the Constitution without having to go through a convention. Proceeding first with that proposal, or the similar but more detailed Amendment Amendment, could be a more effective means than an Article Five convention to achieve such amendments. And, despite his acceptance of using the Article Five state-called convention method to initiate amendments, like other conservatives Levin remains opposed to a general convention unlimited as to subject matter.

### Can the Problems of the Article Five Convention Be Fixed?

The ConConCon was based on the realization that getting 34 states to call for a convention would require support from both liberal and conservative states and legislatures. The ConConCon demonstrated that that will never happen. Conservatives will insist that the convention be limited as to subject, and neither conservatives nor liberals are apt to approve the others' proposed convention topics. But what if by some improbable confluence of events 34 states did submit identical applications for a convention? Then the real trouble would begin, because Article Five is completely silent as to such a convention's procedures, and there is no consensus about how to run one. Of course, lots of people have lots of ideas about how a convention should be run, but they all contradict each other.

Doubts about the convention method are not new. As noted above, James Madison argued throughout the 1787 convention that the lack of any procedures in Article Five would make a convention unworkable. Many states have been willing to issue calls for a convention on particular issues. A few proposals have been passed by 32 or 33 states. However, subsequent states then held back from becoming the 34<sup>th</sup> because of fears of the uncertainties surrounding the prospect of a second convention. (This suggests that if Madison's convention-free proposal had become Article Five, by now constitutional amendments may well have been initiated by the states.)

The scholarly debate over the possible procedures for a second convention shows just how prescient Madison was. The issue of whether a convention could be limited as to subject matter has already been mentioned. Other issues abound. For example, how would votes be allocated at a convention? At the 1787 convention each state had one vote. However, as mentioned above, many object to this in a second convention because of the difference in state populations. Why should Vermont have the same vote as California? But then how do you allocate votes? Many have proposed that the voting correspond to the seats in Congress, but that is still not proportionate to population because the Senate is allocated two Senators to a state regardless of population. Even if you mirror the House of Representatives you are still off because congressional districts follow state lines and do not have equal populations either. To get an exactly equal apportionment you have to either come up with some form of weighted voting or have convention delegate districts cross state lines.

Then there is the issue of how many delegates there should be. The 1787 convention had only 30 to 40 active participants, and barely survived the divergent viewpoints. What would come of a convention with 535 delegates (equal to the number of members of Congress)? Especially, what would result if those 535 delegates were primarily politicians and law professors, the two most likely professions to make up a new constitutional convention?

And on it goes. How would the delegates be selected? By state legislatures as with the 1787 convention, by election by district like members of the U.S. House of Representatives, by election state-wide at-large like U.S. Senators, or by random lottery as proposed by

Professor Levinson? What vote would be required to pass anything at the convention? A simple majority, or something higher like the two thirds Congress is required to reach to launch a constitutional amendment proposal? Should the President or a state governor have veto power over anything involving the convention? Who would pay for the convention? How long would it last? Could Congress refuse to pass a convention's proposal on to the states for ratification? (Article Five requires that a proposal go from the convention back to Congress to determine whether it is to be ratified by state legislatures or special state conventions.)

Then there is the question of who would decide any of these issues. Since they would almost all have to be settled before the convention could meet, the convention itself could not decide them. Many propose that Congress make these decisions. From the 1960s to the 1980s, several bills were introduced by Senators Everett Dirksen, Sam Ervin, and Orrin Hatch to regulate all these matters. Most did not even make it out of committee. More importantly, having Congress decide raises a profound disconnect. The point of the convention method is to enable states to amend the Constitution without congressional interference. Having Congress dictate the minute procedures of the convention is hardly compatible with that objective.

Another answer is to let the courts decide. However, courts do not act proactively. You have to wait for the event to happen and then have someone start a lawsuit over it (someone very well funded by the way). In addition, a 1939 Supreme Court case called *Coleman v. Miller* suggested that the courts should not interfere with the amendment process at all. (*Coleman* was the basis for the courts' rejections of Bill Walker's lawsuits to force Congress to call a constitutional convention.)

The likely scenario, if by some wild chance an Article Five convention were to be called, would be that someone, probably many parties, would immediately sue over many different procedural provisions however they were made by whoever made them. Either the beginning of the convention would be enjoined and delayed for years as the lawsuits wound their way to the Supreme Court, or the convention would start but operate under a persistent doubt as to the validity of anything it did because of the lawsuits.

In short, James Madison was right. Any Article Five convention would be completely unworkable. Further, the turmoil it would create could be a constitutional nightmare. Without clear precedent or rules, many people would always be dissatisfied with the legitimacy of whatever outcome resulted. Which, as Madison noted, is much to be avoided when you are dealing with a Constitution.

# SIX

## Why Democrats, Republicans and Americans Should Support the Amendment Amendment

As the organizers of the ConConCon realized, separately neither progressives nor conservatives can alone meet the current Article Five's two-thirds thresholds against the established political and economic interests which are deeply invested in the current system. Only a coalition of Americans who agree that that system is contrary to the will of the people can prevail against those established interests. We first need to reform Article Five. Afterward progressives and conservatives can present their alternative solutions to the American people, and the people will decide. But, for either set of solutions to go before the people, there must be a means of getting past the vested interests. The Amendment Amendment offers that means if a progressive/conservative coalition can unite long enough to enact it. To realize such a coalition, it balances objectives of both sides with real (but hopefully acceptable) compromises.

States and federalism are profoundly important to conservatives. Decentralizing power away from the national government back to the states and the people is a central tenet of the conservative movement. Any reform which diminishes or abolishes the role of the states will never be supported by conservatives. The Amendment Amendment respects the states' role by preserving state equality in voting (as well as enabling the states to amend without having to deal with the archaic mechanism of a convention).

On the other hand, a central tenet of progressivism is to enhance direct popular participation in government. Initiative, referendum and recall were all created by the early progressive movement. The Amendment Amendment advances this goal by introducing referenda for the first time into the federal Constitution. Many conservatives steeped in constitutional history will quickly cite the framers' deep distrust of direct democracy, and the many structural barriers they put in place to moderate popular enthusiasms. The expression that the "United States is a republic, not a democracy" is an article of faith to a significant portion of the conservative faithful. Although the Amendment Amendment limits them to the state level and makes them subject to state legislatures' discretion, the introduction of referenda into the Constitution would represent a significant compromise for these conservative constitutionalists.

Progressives and conservatives also each have their own strategic reasons to support the Amendment Amendment. Conservatives strongly believe that, until very recently, the Supreme Court has been making decisions contrary to the Constitution's original meaning. Our legal system is based on a concept called *stare decisis*, which requires judges to follow prior decisions. This conservative concept is fundamental to the rule of law, because it permits us to know what the law is and plan for the future accordingly. However, historically *stare decisis* just served to lock in previous unconstitutional Supreme Court precedents. While conservatives may wish that *stare decisis* will now protect the current Supreme Court's more constitutionally solid decisions, realism tells us that those will be blown away as soon as the political winds turn and control of the judiciary passes again to progressives whose regard for *stare decisis* is only opportunistic. (Recently many progressives have become *stare decisis* enthusiasts as the Supreme Court's new conservative majority has overturned many previous progressive decisions such as *Roe v. Wade*.)

And there is a more fundament argument from principle to be considered. During the long decades of progressive domination of the Supreme Court and federal judiciary, constitutional conservatives railed against the free-handed disregard of the Constitution practiced by those judges. These constitutionalists argued that the question was not particular outcomes, but rather the unconstitutionally expanded power of the judiciary. Even when the judiciary rules in ways they consider correct, for true constitutional conservatives, constitutional amendment, not judicial activism, is the proper way to restore the Constitution's original meaning and limits on the federal government.

Progressives who have looked to the Supreme Court to move America toward greater social justice and equality face a stark future. Donald Trump's appointment of three Supreme Court justices has created a solid six justice conservative majority on the Supreme Court, and with Republican control of the Presidency and the Senate following the 2024 election, it is highly likely that the Supreme Court will be dominated by conservatives for a long time to come. Moving forward, an effective constitutional amendment process is now going to be the only avenue for implementing any other progressive constitutional reform, or counteracting decisions of a newly conservative dominated Supreme Court.

Of course, this is not to say that there should be a constitutional amendment every time one disagrees with a Supreme Court decision. But the existence of this realistic check will safeguard against future runaway judicial activism in either direction. And some structural constitutional changes, such as a balanced budget mandate, electing the President by majority of the popular vote, or term limits on Congress and the Supreme Court, are beyond even the greatest judicial creativity, and would have to be enacted by constitutional amendment.

### *A Left – Right Alliance to Return our Constitution to the People?*

At a time when the nation's divisions were even fiercer than ours today, Lincoln asked that Americans not be "enemies, but friends," and that political passions not "break our bonds of affection." The last sentence of his first inaugural is often invoked, his plea that the "mystic chords of memory, stretching from every battle-field, and patriot grave, to every living heart and hearthstone, all over this broad land, will yet swell the chorus of the Union, when again touched, as surely they will be, by the better angels of our nature."

Americans ignored his plea then, and perhaps it was and is unrealistic to expect that political opponents have "bonds of affection" for each other. We usually think of progressives and conservatives, of left and right, as irreconcilable opposites. However, let me suggest a different perspective. It is the concept of center and periphery. This concept comes from development economics, in which underdevelopment is explained by continuing control of resources by the center. Economic activity is forced to pass through the center where a large part of the value added is siphoned off before being recycled back to peripheral regions. This concept is applicable in international contexts, where the center is former colonial powers, or nationally, where the center is a capital megacity.

Whatever one thinks of the concept as economics, it can have a lot of explanatory power when applied to modern American politics. A complex of intertwined government and business interests control our national government. A revolving door cycles the same people as legislators, bureaucrats, and lobbyists through the power centers of Wall Street and K Street. Domineering federal bureaucrats and bailed-out derivatives traders are both cogs in the machine. The "inside-the-Beltway" wings of both political parties are deeply immersed in this center, as is the mainstream media. Left out of this center are most Americans, who are the periphery. Progressives tend to see the Big Business side of this complex, and conservatives the Big Government side, but could they both be simply observing the same thing, this American power center, from different perspectives in the periphery?

The development economists' solution to the center-periphery trap was to promote direct trade amongst the regions of the periphery. Perhaps the same solution might help address our national situation.

Although they could not agree on something as indeterminate and amorphous as a second constitutional convention, the dialogue and the civility of the ConConCon suggests that direct action amongst the people of the periphery which bypasses the power center is possible, if not on a global program, but at least to achieve specific common goals. To the horror of the so-called "moderate" center, could "outside-the-Beltway" American progressives and conservatives talk to each other, even work together to give We the People a say in our Constitution? Such alliances have been imagined. Ralph Nader, for example, has actively encouraged such strategies, which he calls "convergences."

If both progressives and conservatives demand it, it is really possible that two-thirds of the House and Senate would vote to approve the Amendment Amendment. Even though it would open an end run around it, Congress is not using its power to initiate amendments in any case. Who in Congress would oppose a proposal which is all about "power-to-the-people," but is also content-neutral and only procedural? Members of Congress could support the Amendment Amendment without having to commit themselves to any particular subsequent amendment proposal. Indeed, most members of Congress claim to support various amendment proposals, and could present their support of the Amendment Amendment as a way of advancing those proposals. Finally, since the Amendment Amendment would vest state legislatures with a significant new constitutional role, ratification by three fourths of the states should readily follow.

The Amendment Amendment seeks to balance the goods of both popular participation and of federalism. Neither progressives nor conservatives are expected to wholeheartedly embrace its concessions to the other, or each other's possible amendment proposals. However, this balance could permit a temporary alliance for a common goal, to enact the Amendment Amendment restoring control of our Constitution to the true source of its authority – we the people of the United States.

# APPENDIX

## Text of Article V as revised by the Amendment Amendment

Section 1:     This Constitution may be amended by either: (a) five eighths of both Houses of Congress and five eighths of the States, which approvals by the Congress and the States may occur concurrently, or (b) two thirds of the States with a majority of the nation's population as determined by the most recent Enumeration made pursuant to Article I Section 2 of this Constitution prior to the completion of the procedures set forth in this Section. If the first approval of a proposed amendment is by States, at least five States must approve the proposed amendment within a period of not more than one hundred twenty calendar days. Each State may determine whether actions under this article are to be by its legislature or by referendum.

Section 2:     All approvals of any proposed amendment shall expire if the proposed amendment has not been fully approved (a) for proposed amendments initiated by the Congress seven calendar years after the vote of whichever House of Congress was the first to approve it, or (b) for proposed amendments initiated by States nine calendar years after the first State approval.

Section 3:     The operative text of any amendment must be approved with identical wording.

Section 4:     Congress and any State may rescind approval of a proposed amendment except during the thirty calendar days prior to the date upon which the proposed amendment is fully approved under Section 1 of this article.

Section 5:     An amendment shall be valid to all intents and purposes as part of this Constitution upon completion of the procedures set out in Section 1 of this article unless the amendment itself sets a future effective date. An approval or rescission of an approval of a proposed amendment shall be effective upon the completion of Congress' or a State's procedures for ordinary legislative or ballot actions, or as the legislature or a State's constitution may otherwise provide, except that no executive assent, veto or other action shall apply to any action under this article other than the conduct and certification of referenda hereunder.

Section 6: Congress' and each State's approvals and rescissions of approvals of proposed amendments must be promptly transmitted to the Speaker of the House of Representatives, who must within seven calendar days of receipt: (a) publicly post all such actions, (b) transmit them to the Senate and the legislatures of the States, and (c) declare the enactment of an amendment upon fulfillment of the requirements of this article. In the event of any failure to perform an executory action under this article, upon the application of any member of Congress, or with respect to any State any member of that State's legislature, the courts constituted under Article III of this Constitution must decree such action to be effected.

Section 7: No amendment shall deprive any State of its equal suffrage in the Senate without its consent.